Vikings
of the West

A WHO · WHEN · WHERE BOOK

Vikings
of the West

The Scandinavian Immigrants in America

Written by Ruth Holland

Pictures by H. B. Vestal

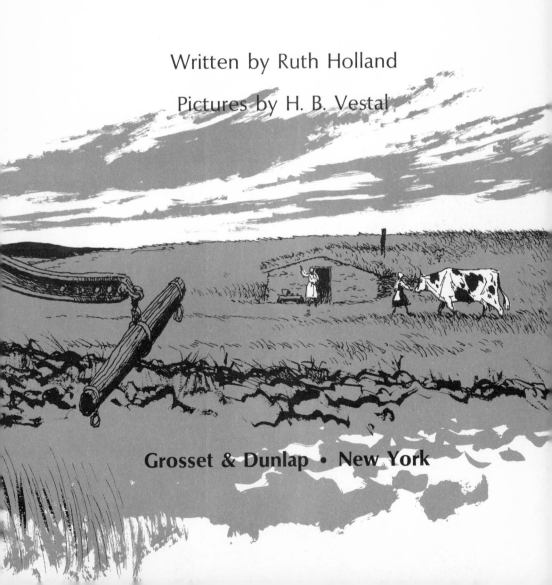

Grosset & Dunlap • New York

Introduction

The countries of Norway, Sweden, Finland and Denmark were visited by a strange kind of epidemic during most of the nineteenth century and to some extent well into the twentieth. Known as "America Fever," it could be diagnosed largely from observation. The signs were unmistakeable — flushed cheeks, bright eyes and a voice bubbling over with enthusiasm. There was an overwhelming urge in the stricken one to travel to a faraway land of opportunity, no matter what the cost in funds or hardship. There were also recurring dreams of a huge farm, acres of grain and herds of cattle.

"America Fever" spread from person to person, faster than the common cold. No man, woman or child seemed to be immune. Peasants on farms and fishermen and their families in scores of coastal villages appeared to be particularly susceptible.

Many factors contributed to this wave of restlessness and ambition. The rugged, rocky lands of northern Europe, while lending themselves to magnificent scenic beauty, could not alone produce enough in crops to feed their people. At the same time, stories of America's wealth and land resources, glowingly proclaimed by newspapers, posters and the letters of friends and relatives who had already ventured forth, held untold promise and could hardly be ignored. And perhaps more than anything else, there was Ole Rynnig's *America Book,* replete with instructions and suggestions, an indispensable guide for journeying to the New World. Dog-eared, thumbed-through pages attested to its constant reference and study by all who could buy, borrow or beg a copy.

Were it not for "America Fever" and its "cure," the actual immigration of the Scandinavian people, the United States would have lacked much in its progressive growth. The descendants of the vikings brought with them much-needed skills in lumbering and fishing, and especially in farming and dairying. Their story (and that of their great contributions to their adopted land) is told with sympathy and simplicity in this book, providing fascinating, informative reading from beginning to end.

Library of Congress Catalog Card Number: 67-23801

CONTENTS

CHAPTER I

Prairie Christmas, 1868

Somewhere out on a desolate, wind-torn prairie, like lonely ships tossed by a cruel sea, four huts had been cut from the soil, each one sheltering a family. "Sod houses," without windows, without doors, dirt roofs, dirt floors.

The sod was the good, black, rich earth of northwestern America. It was the fertile land the settlers had journeyed so long to find. They had expected to arrive in the spring, in time to plant grain and reap rich harvests. They had expected to grow pasture land for their livestock. The calf and the bull they'd bought with their last few dollars would breed and grow into a herd of cattle. Life would be good and rich like the good earth itself. The children would grow tall and strong. The family would flourish. And all, all of this, would come from the land.

But so far the land had given them nothing. Nothing except for the sod patches they'd cut from the ground to make a roof over their heads. They had arrived too late in the year for planting. It was September before they had chosen their sites — just time enough to build the four sod houses before the snows came.

Now it was Christmas Eve in the year 1868. Inside one of the sod houses Olaf Sorensen was wondering if just this night they might not spare an extra log for the fire. An extravagance, a gift to the children and to Kjersti, his wife, for Christmas. They had not exchanged gifts. They had not sung their Christmas songs. There was not even grain enough to put out for the birds.

Back home in Norway, throwing seeds into the wind so that not even the birds would be forgotten was a part of the Christmas tradition the children had loved. But the Yule Buck was *really* the best part. He came in the night and left Christmas treasures to find the next morning. Perhaps a spinning top, or a toy sailboat, or an embroidered apron just like Mamma's. The older children could remember how Christmas had been back home in Norway.

Peder Sorensen happily remembered counting off the days until Christmas Eve. From the kitchen came the warm smell of flat bread and roasting duck. His mother and his grandmother bustled about, cheerfully scolding his little sister, Sorinna, for getting in their way. Peder was nine years old when they'd left Norway. Now he was twelve, but there were many things he still remembered.

He could remember a house made of wood, not dirt. He could remember, before they came out here to live, eat, sleep and cook in this one dirt room, that once there had been a house with many rooms — one room for cooking, another for eating, and still another just for sleeping. He remembered the taste of porridge and flat bread and a sip of beer from his father's cup. His mother had been happy then, pretty and smiling. The neighbors called her "Olaf's beauty," and someday, they said, when little Sorinna grew up, she would be the image of her mother. Then Olaf Sorensen would have two beauties and four sons, strong, brave and adventurous, like their father.

Hans, the eldest, was a young man of eighteen now. Next came Simon, tall and strong and quiet. He was only sixteen, but to twelve-year-old Peder he seemed a full-grown man. Then, after Peder, came the little ones, Tomaas and Sorinna. Peder wondered sometimes whether eight-year-old Tomaas looked up to him as he did to Simon and Hans. Sorinna was only seven.

"Yes," Olaf decided. "I will do it. I will keep the fire warm just a little bit longer. For the children, for Kjersti and for Christmas."

As he stepped away from the fast dwindling woodpile, he caught the angry look on Kjersti's face.

"So," thought Olaf, "I was wrong. Will I never be able to make her happy again? She is angry because of the cold, but if I add wood to the fire she is still angrier. She hates it here. She hates this hut which she cannot call a house. The dirt cave, she calls it. 'We are living in a dirt cave,' she wrote home to her mother in Norway."

Olaf had persuaded Kjersti to come. She'd been frightened to leave her parents, her friends and her church. Frightened to cross the ocean to this strange land where no one spoke Norwegian. How would she manage?

"You will learn English," Olaf promised.

What about the children? Where would they go to school? Would there be a minister to teach them the religion of their forefathers?

"The children will be Lutheran, just as we are. But, they will be American, too. One person can be many things in a free country," Olaf persuaded.

Three years had gone by since then. Three years so hard, so cruel, so painful that Olaf was afraid to look back. If the years to come were just as bad . . . No, No. He could not afford to think like that. If he did, his fear might destroy him. He *must* look ahead! This endless winter would end.

Spring would bring the first warm days. They would plant their first crop. The corn would come up tall and yellow. And, as far as the eye could see, there would be fields of wheat, an ocean of feathery grain swaying in the gentle prairie breeze. And overhead, the sun would provide warmth. Olaf pictured Sorinna and Tomaas running, rolling in the grass underneath a perfect, hot, yellow sun. He thought the ice might finally leave his bones. He would stretch his legs and his arms pulling the plough, breaking the soil, planting the seeds, under a hot, hot sun.

Outside, the earth was blanketed with snow and still more was coming down. Olaf guessed it must be over four feet deep. It had been this way for weeks.

There was still a little wood left. After it was gone, they planned to twist hay into bundles to feed the fire.

But the three other families? How were they doing? Did they have food enough or fuel enough to stay alive? What was happening to them out in this wilderness?

Four families had come from Norway together: the Sorensens, the Petersons, the Hansens and the Tonsetens.

It had taken them three years to cross the ocean and the land. By boat, by foot and by prairie wagon they'd travelled the endless plain. Could anyone know the vastness of this land? From Illinois, through Iowa, Nebraska, North Dakota, South Dakota and Minnesota they wandered, looking for the perfect spot. The plain stretched — how it stretched — south to Kansas and far north into Canada. It seemed to have no beginning, no middle and no end. Blizzards hurled snow from a gray sky. The wind was a monster, howling with rage.

But Olaf insisted that one day it would stop. Then they would be able to see how the others were, the others in their separate sod houses, snowed in as the Sorensens were.

"Soon, very soon it will stop."

No one answered.

Olaf turned to his littlest children, Sorinna and Tomaas.

"Your brothers and I will make you some snowshoes and then we'll go out visiting. How happy our friends will be to see us and how happy we'll be to see them."

The children were delighted with the idea of snowshoes. Peder, Hans and Simon couldn't resist their father's optimism.

"Yes," enthusiastic Peder agreed. "The others are all certainly fine, except for perhaps worrying about us."

"Merry Christmas," said Sorinna, quite suddenly.

They all laughed except Kjersti.

"Mamma," Sorinna pleaded, trying to make her mother join the group, "I think I remember something from Norway. I think I remember a blue dress. I wore it on the boat and I had it awhile in America, too. Do I remember right, Mamma?"

Kjersti looked first at her daughter, then at her husband. "Yes. Your grandmother made it. It was blue as the fjords of Norway. I must remember too, because I will never see those blue waters again. Never again."

Olaf tried to bring back the lighthearted mood of a moment ago. "Maybe next Christmas the Yule Buck will bring you another blue dress." He winked at Sorinna.

His wife turned on him. "And you, Olaf," Kjersti cried. "What do you remember? To persuade poor Sorinna that she will have a new dress, just so that she may be disappointed again? Do you remember the *America Book* Olaf? Or are you still too full of 'America fever'?"

CHAPTER II

The America Fever

The symptoms were easy to recognize. No one needed to call in a doctor to diagnose a case of the "America fever." Flushed cheeks, eager eyes and voice bubbling with enthusiasm were the first signs. And, if the person also felt an immense restlessness, an overpowering need to be off and away to a new world, if he dreamed at night of a huge farm, acres of grain, herds of cattle, well, that was it! Another Scandinavian down with a severe case of the "America fever."

No doubt about it. There was a new kind of epidemic spreading from Norway to Sweden, from Sweden to Denmark, from Denmark to Finland.

These beautiful, rugged, rocky lands of northern Europe simply did not have enough fertile soil to feed all their people. The population grew, but the land did not. Now there seemed a way out. Across the ocean there was a new country — America — where land could be had for the asking. It seemed too good to be true, and yet it must be so. The stories of America's riches were printed in the newspapers, advertised on posters, came by mail from friends and relatives already there.

And so "America fever" spread, from person to person, from family to family.

In Norway people poured over the pages of Ole

Rynnig's *America Book*. Some who could not read learned whole pages by heart. The real title of the book was *A True Account of America for the Information and Help of Peasant and Commoner*, but it came to be known far and wide simply as the *America Book*.

Ole Rynnig arrived in America in 1837. He was a well educated, well-to-do young man, who could easily have stayed on in Norway and become a minister, like his father. He could have lived comfortably and never troubled himself at all about the world outside his front door. But he was extremely depressed by the poverty he saw all around him. Norway was overpopulated. A man could barely catch enough fish or grow enough food to feed his family. Taxes were high and the people were growing more and more discouraged.

"A great and good idea formed the central point of all his thinking," Ole's fellow immigrant Ansten Nattestad wrote. "He hoped to be able to provide the poor, oppressed Norwegian workman with a happier home on this side of the sea, and to realize this wish, he shunned no sacrifice."

In 1837 Ole Rynnig organized a group of eighty-four farmers to come with him to America. They travelled across unsettled country to Illinois where, seventy miles south of a small town called Chicago, they set up their village. They called it Beaver Creek.

The immigrants chopped down trees and built log cabins like the ones peasants lived in back home. They planted and harvested. Ole kept a record of their adventure and when his book was complete, Ansten Nattestad brought it back to Norway to be published.

In Sweden people heard of the *America Book,* and a Swedish copy was printed. Swedes, Danes and Norwegians all read the book. This was the beginning of the "America fever."

A young Swede, Gustav Unonius, helped it along. In 1840, Unonius, a government official in the university town of Uppsala, decided to bring his bride to America because "a workman has the same right to citizenship as anyone else. Work, in any industry that is honorable, is no shame in America."

Three friends asked to come along with Unonius and his wife and their maid. Six passengers in all, they paid twenty-six dollars apiece for their tickets, and set sail for America. They landed in New York and travelled west until they reached Wisconsin. There, about twenty miles from Milwaukee, they found a place that reminded them of home. A forest of evergreens led down to a sandy lake shore. New Uppsala, they called it.

Unlike Ole Rynnig's group, Unonius' little band of six didn't have one experienced farmer among them. New Uppsala was beautiful enough, but the soil was not fertile. Occasionally, new settlers would arrive, but they soon drifted off again to look for better land elsewhere. The colony lasted ten years, but Unonius returned to Sweden long before then. Strangely enough, it didn't seem to matter a bit that he was bitterly disappointed in America. The land had not yielded crops, and he thought that the religious freedom and democracy were dangerous.

The Swedish farmers, hungry for land and a better life, ignored what Unonius said after he returned. They heard only what they wanted to hear. They remembered his old

letters from America to a Swedish newspaper, *Aftonbladet*, when he wrote:

"The people here have *everything*. . . . The land is beautiful, adorned with oak woods and prairies broken by rivers, and lakes swarming with fish. . . . The soil is fertile and wonderful, and usually consists of rich black mold. . . . As for us, we do not regret our undertaking. We are leading

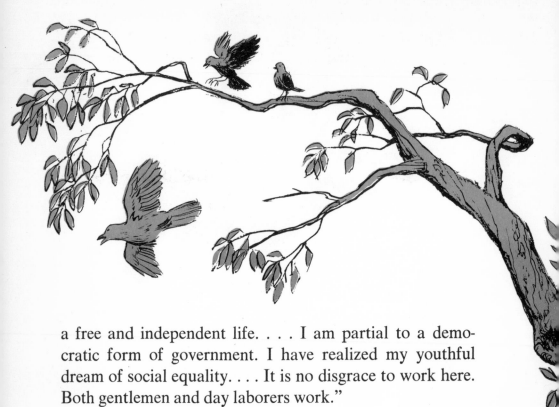

a free and independent life. . . . I am partial to a democratic form of government. I have realized my youthful dream of social equality. . . . It is no disgrace to work here. Both gentlemen and day laborers work."

The "America fever" spread.

In 1849 Frederika Bremer, Sweden's leading writer, decided to have a look at America for herself. She arrived in New York and travelled west, following the Swedish communities. As a famous writer, she was welcomed everywhere, and got to meet many prominent Americans. She was a friendly, curious sort of person who asked an astounding number of questions. She kept a diary which was published in 1853 in the form of letters to a sister. They became the most influential *America letters* in Sweden. Because they were so sympathetic to the American spirit and America's problems, they were translated into English and became an instant best-seller in America as well as in Sweden.

"What a glorious new Scandinavia might not Minnesota become," she wrote. "Here the Swede would find his clear, romantic lakes, the plains of Skane rich in grain, and the valleys of Norrland. Here the Norwegian would find his rapid rivers, his lofty mountains. The Danes might pasture their flocks and herds and lay out their farms on richer and less misty coasts than those of Denmark."

Like most Scandinavians, Frederika Bremer was opposed to slavery on religious and moral grounds. Her *America letters* were quite outspoken in their contempt for a system that enriched one man by enslaving many others. Not only were young Swedes inspired by her letters to leave home and try their hand at farming in Minnesota, but when the Civil War broke out, they were invariably found fighting on the Union side.

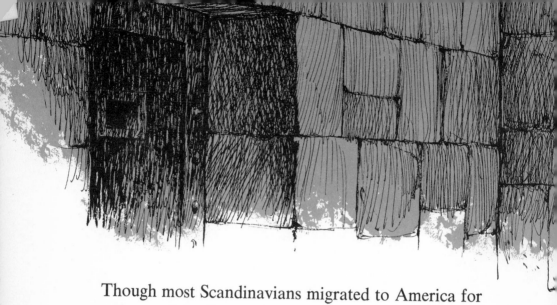

Though most Scandinavians migrated to America for economic reasons, there were those who came in search of other things. Sweden, Norway and Denmark were ruled by kings and noblemen. The son of a fisherman would undoubtedly be a fisherman, like his father and grandfather before him. The son of a tenant farmer could do no more than dream of owning his own land. There was very little chance that his dream would come true. A poor farmer, fisherman or workman could not expect to send his children to a university to have them study a profession and raise their position in the world. His children and his children's children would be bowing and scraping and tipping their hats to noblemen all their lives, just as he had done.

But in the New World there were no noblemen. The people chose their own leaders. The children of immigrant fathers would be citizens of the United States. They would vote in elections. Though their farms might be small or poor, their legal rights would be equal to those of the richest landowner.

Still other Scandinavians, like those first immigrants from England who landed at Plymouth Rock, came in search of religious freedom.

The Scandinavian countries had one established "state religion" — Lutheranism. The rulers supported the Lutheran Church and the Lutheran Church supported the rulers. Even if a Scandinavian were not Lutheran, part of his taxes still went to support the state church. Anyone who said anything against the official church would be going against the law of the land. He might even end up in jail, as Eric Jansson did.

Eric Jansson had been imprisoned several times because of his opposition to the Lutheran Church of Sweden. Finally, in 1846, he fled to America where he and his followers established one of the most successful Swedish immigrant communities in the New World. Jansson named their settlement Bishop's Hill, after the town of Biskop-skulla, near the farm where he was born.

Although Jansson was the son of a poor tenant farmer, somehow he learned to read and write. One of the few books available to him as a boy was the Bible and perhaps that's what started his early passion for religion. The long, lonely, Swedish winter nights provided a great deal of time for him to study the Bible.

When Jansson would leave the farm and go into town, he was horrified by what he saw. His fellow Lutherans were "drinking and sinning." He advised them to repent and their sins would be washed away. He was an enormously power-ful speaker. His eyes burned with religious zeal and he soon attracted many followers.

He and his disciples were convinced that the only real writing about God was in the Bible. So, on June 11, 1844, they built a huge bonfire and burned all the books dealing with religion, except the Bible. This was a violation of Swedish law and Jansson was sent to prison. He held many such book-burnings, and each time he was sent to jail. Each time he got out he found that his group of disciples had grown. Jansson told them he was a special representa-tive of God, whose will was revealed to him directly. He had an almost hypnotic effect on his audiences; those who believed in him followed him blindly. When the government became more severe towards him, hysteria and violence broke out.

Jansson's emigration from Sweden was something of a joke. With police looking for him everywhere, he disguised himself as a woman and skied out of Sweden. A year and

a half later, Jansson and his family and a group of followers arrived in New York.

Unlike Unonius' choice of settlement in New Uppsala,
the Janssonists chose a perfect place for their colony. On
August 21, 1846, they bought a complete farm in Henry
County, Illinois. They paid $1,100 for 156 acres with farm-
house, barns and livestock included. In September they
bought another 480 acres from the government, at $1.25
an acre.

The Janssonists lived by strict rules of community
property. Before they left Sweden they sold what they

owned and turned all the money over to their leaders. All were equal partners in the community.

The first years at Bishop's Hill were not easy. Most of the settlers lived in tents. When it got too cold for tents, they moved to dugouts in the sides of a ravine. Each dugout was about thirty feet long. It held forty to fifty double-decker bunks of rough planks. The ceilings were made of logs covered with sod. A single fireplace was built at one end.

They had no doctor, no drugs, no experienced neighbor to call upon for help. Supplies dwindled until there was almost nothing left to eat. Then Jansson declared certain days each week as religious "fast days." That helped stretch the food a little longer.

Each morning the settlers awoke at four thirty. Prayer meeting began at five, and for two hours they stood in the cold praying with their leader for deliverance and salvation. By spring there were no more boards left to make coffins. Cold, hunger, pneumonia, dysentery, cholera and

malaria had taken so many of the settlers that they began to bury their dead in mass graves.

In the spring of 1847 they broke ground for their first crop. Each year they broke more ground, planted more seed and reaped a larger harvest. By 1855 Bishop's Hill colony owned 109 horses, over 1,000 pigs, 586 head of cattle, plus geese, chickens and turkeys. They raised corn, rye, barley and wheat. They grew fields of flax that they spun into yarn and wove into linen cloth and rugs.

By 1859 they owned 8,500 acres, and their property was valued at $770,000. They made their clothes from the ground up — grew the plant, spun the wool and wove the cloth. They tanned leather and made their own shoes; they chopped down trees and milled lumber in their own mills; they made bricks by hand for their new homes. Some of these sturdy frame and brick houses are still standing today.

During this time the settlers sent their "America letters" back home. What fabulous tales these were! They were read and re-read, passed from hand to hand, and finally even published in the newspapers. Many people, hearing the news from Bishop's Hill, set out for America. But they did not head for Eric Jansson's colony. They had heard that he ruled with an iron fist, and that he was, in fact, a dictator. They wanted to try the experiment on their own, to break the land, grow the crops and raise their children in freedom, not under Jansson's thumb.

In 1850 Jansson was assassinated by one of his own colonists. Despite its success, there was dissatisfaction at Bishop's Hill. Some people resented Jansson's power; others resented not being allowed to own their own property. Quite a few families left the colony to homestead on their own. The anger and resentment grew until it erupted in Jansson's violent death.

But no matter what happened at Bishop's Hill, the "America letters" had done their job. "America fever" spread faster than the common cold. It spread from the peasants on the farms to the coastal fishing villages.

Scandinavians had been dependent upon the sea from the time of the Vikings. Since the cold, rocky, barren land yielded little, they took most of their food from the sea and the fjords. But winter always brought violent storms and angry seas. The ocean claimed many a fisherman who was out in pursuit of his livelihood.

Norwegian fishermen poured over the *America Book*. For centuries their families had lived in coastal villages and led a seafaring life. But perhaps the time had come to turn their backs on the sea for the safety and security of a new land as vast and rich as the ocean.

Ole Rynnig, Frederika Bremer, Unonius and the "America letters" told stories of adventure and success in America. One after another, the descendants of the Vikings decided to try their hand at the inland life.

The "America fever" spread.

CHAPTER III

Free Land

The "America letters" and Ole Rynnig's *America Book* were inspiration enough for thousands of struggling Scandinavians. But for those who still hesitated, there was another, more powerful persuader. Beginning in 1867, Sweden and Norway were hit with three terrible years of crop failure. The famine began in northern Sweden, spread south to include all of Sweden and, finally, Norway.

Farmers without crops could not feed their families or pay taxes on their land. They lost their farms and took to the roads which were crowded with poor, homeless families begging for food. The price of food soared out of a poor man's reach and thousands were starving.

Scandinavian immigrants in America did what they could. Money was raised to send a shipload of grain to Sweden. Some immigrants could even afford to send tickets

for America to their relatives back home. They had survived the first few years of hardship. They had cut farms out of uncultivated land. They had not remained in the eastern seaport cities where their boats docked, as so many other immigrants had. They had pushed on. With the strength and courage to try and tame a wilderness, they had pushed westward by foot, by boat, and by covered wagon. They were the ideal pioneers.

Much as the Scandinavians needed the land, the land needed the Scandinavians. Who else would turn the vast territory west of Chicago into the states of Iowa, Minnesota, South Dakota, North Dakota, Washington and Oregon? Who would breed the cattle, farm the land, cut down the forests and mill the lumber? Why, the men who played the "Swedish fiddle," of course. You didn't need to be Scandinavian to play the "Swedish fiddle." There were others who helped conquer the West, but so many were Scandinavian that the cheerful ring of an ax against a tree, of a saw cutting lumber, came to be known as the music of the "Swedish fiddle."

The American government began to advertise for Scandinavians. Wisconsin competed with Iowa, Iowa with Illinois, Illinois with Kansas. States hired agents to help them lure Scandinavians to western America.

Iowa printed a pamphlet to be distributed in Sweden, Norway and Denmark, called "Iowa, the Home for Immigrants."

Wisconsin and Kansas ran ads in Scandinavian newspapers.

North and South Dakota tried an original approach. They appealed to the women. They advertised free homesteads and "other attractions that will soon find you a mate."

In 1862 Congress passed the Homestead Act. It offered 160 acres of land free to any farmer who would clear it and improve it.

Free land. Hungry, homeless famine victims, wandering the roads of Sweden and Norway in search of a day's work in exchange for some grain, saw posters nailed up on trees. They were wooed by agents sent over from the new territories. Everywhere they heard the same thing: "In America, there is land — free land for anyone willing to work it."

American businessmen advertised, too. The steamship companies, the canal boats, the new railroad all needed passengers. They knew that few farmers could afford to pay for tickets, so they offered an exchange. Free passage for a man and his family to America in exchange for a year's work once he got here. They put out little pamphlets showing where free land was available. They called this country the "land of opportunity," where a man could educate his children, own property, and be proud of his labor. America advertised her charms boldly and loudly.

What more persuasion did a poor Scandinavian need? He wanted to come, and he was wanted here.

"And now farewell to all my folk and parish,
For I am going to America,
To seek a happier life in the New World.
There is no help for it,
I must cross the sea.
Life here has become too hard for me."

This was the popular song of the day, as family after family was swept up in the "America fever."

Throughout the 1870's and 1880's, more and more Swedes emigrated. So many farmers left that the Swedish government became concerned. In 1882 the Swedish Parliament tried to pass a law to prevent people from leaving. After all, they needed some "Swedish fiddlers," too. But the law was not passed and thousands more left Sweden for America.

When the great Swedish migration was over, one million, two hundred thousand Swedes had set up homes in the New World. This was a third of the entire Swedish population at that time.

Between 1820 and 1865, seventy-eight thousand Norwegians emigrated. Between 1866 and 1873, one hundred and eleven thousand more settled in the United States.

Three hundred and fifty thousand immigrants came to America from Denmark.

What started as just a handful of adventurers in the

1820's grew to include thousands in the 1840's. By the end
of the Civil War, in 1865, ten thousand Scandinavians a
year were emigrating to the United States.

It's hard to imagine how the American West could
possibly have been settled without them.

They cleared and cultivated over ten million acres of land — two million acres in Minnesota alone. Entire counties in Wisconsin, Illinois, Kansas and the Dakotas are made up almost entirely of descendants of Scandinavian immigrants.

In 1880 a Swede, Carl de Laval, invented the first cream separator. Shortly afterwards a Danish immigrant brought it with him to the New World, which revolutionized the American dairy industry. It was then possible to produce butter and cheese that was both cheap and of good quality. In the American dairy land of Wisconsin and Minnesota, there are still many districts where all the dairies are owned and run by American descendants of Danish immigrants.

Some of the Norwegian fishermen tried their hands at farming and failed. Others simply could not get used to being so far from the sea. The land could not hold them, so they packed up and headed west again, toward the shores of the Pacific. Here, with their knowledge and love of the sea, they developed western shipbuilding, fishing, and fish canning into mighty industries.

Immigrants who fled from starvation at home built one of the richest farm lands in the world out of our American West. It was painfully hard, back-breaking work. There were many bleak years and many long, cold winter nights, like the Christmas Eve in 1868 when the Sorensens huddled around a small fire in their sod hut, remembering home. But they were settled in, and in spring they would plant.

At last the trip lay behind them.

CHAPTER IV

By Land and By Sea to the New World

Soup for the Seasick
Sulphur Powder for the Itch
An Iron Plate for Cooking Flatbread
Dried Meat
Dried Fish
Butter
Cheese
Beer
Flour
Peas
Cereals
Potatoes
Rye Husks
Coffee
Tea
Sugar
Brandy
Vinegar
Wine
Linen
Salt Water Soap
Fine Combs.

These are just a few of the provisions Ole Rynnig advised immigrants to bring along for the trip.

The Sorensens and their neighbors had pored over the

list. No one would think of making so hazardous a voyage without consulting Ole Rynnig's guide. At best, the trip would last twelve weeks. But there was always a chance of foul weather. Storms at sea might blow the ship off course and it could be four or five months before they reached America. Even after the invention of the steamboat, crossing the Atlantic took weeks in the 1860's and 1870's.

A family needed to plan carefully many, many months in advance for such a journey so that they would be sure to arrive in America at just the right time.

"The best time to leave," Ole Rynnig wrote, "is so early in the spring as to be able to reach the place of settlement by midsummer. In that way, something can be raised even the first year, namely buckwheat which is planted in the last days of June, turnips which are planted in the latter part of July, and potatoes. It is very unfortunate to go too late in the year to gather fodder for one or two cows and build a house for the winter."

But what most immigrants could not possibly imagine was the enormous journey still ahead of them after they reached America. Norway, Sweden and Denmark are small countries; Sweden, the largest of the Scandinavian countries, is smaller than the state of Texas. How could these Scandinavians possibly picture the barren plain that stretched more than a thousand miles from Ohio to Wyoming? No matter how carefully they planned, there were bound to be unexpected delays. If the ship were blown off course, they would be late. If they ran out of money before they found a homesite, they would need to stop and find work. If a child fell ill, if they lost their way crossing the prairie, or if they searched too long for the ideal spot to settle, they would be late — too late to plant a first crop and build a warm house for winter.

They made painstaking plans. First, a man must sell what he could to raise money for the trip. The best way was to hold an auction sale for his neighbors, who were remaining behind, to buy up his possessions. If he owned a bit of land, he sold it. He sold his house, his furniture, his farm animals. He sold his sled and his stove and his wife's spinning wheel. Some of these things were hard to part with, like the cradle he had built for his first-born child, or the rocker his grandfather had made for his bride. Still, one after another, they all went up for sale. He needed every kroner he could get. In America, he would exchange kroners for dollars to buy a wagon, a plough, a horse, and a cow.

He kept just a few possessions. Ole Rynnig advised it. A good scythe and a broadax for clearing the land. Lights and bed linens for the trip and, later on, for his new home.

His wife was busy, too. She sewed and spun and knitted new clothes for the entire family. She made quilts and warm coats. She preserved the fish and the meat they would eat on the journey.

If she could, she persuaded her husband not to sell the churn. After all, they would be in America soon. The cow they would buy would give milk and she would make fresh butter from the milk (if they did not sell the churn).

Then, when all was sold and settled, they built the trunk that would travel halfway around the world with them, carrying their most precious possessions. It was made of the strongest lumber they could find, held together by heavy iron hinges. They painted it brilliant shades of red and blue and decorated it with the traditional Scandinavian designs of birds and leaves and flowers. The name and the year were painted boldly across the top. Into the trunk went all the treasures they simply could not bear to leave behind — an old wedding picture, a bridal gown, or a christening robe.

The trunk needed to be sturdy for the tossing about it would get. And so did the people.

Those who lived inland travelled to the nearest fjord by sled. There they changed from sled to sailboat and sailed up the fjord to reach the sea. Here they changed

again. They left the fjord boat to board an ocean-going vessel. Very often this ship had not yet arrived, or it lay out in the harbor many weeks before sailing. The immigrants too poor to pay for lodgings camped out on the docks.

Sometimes, they discovered, it would be months before another ship set sail for America. In that case, they loaded up their possessions once again and travelled across Europe to France or England. There was always a better chance of finding passage aboard an English ship, since England and America were trading with each other.

Ole Rynnig's *America Book* had warned them to be careful of the water aboard ship. It was the captain's job to provide enough water for each person and to see that it was stored in good, clean casks. "If the water in the cask is spoiled," he wrote, "the good water is to be used up before beginning with the bad, and the captain shall take water for his own use from the same barrel as the passengers."

Despite all these precautions, they still ran out of pure water. Passengers fell ill and contagion spread rapidly in

the overcrowded living quarters below decks. The very
young and the very old were the most frequent victims.
Cholera, typhus, influenza and pneumonia were dread dis-
eases in those days, before the discovery of modern drugs
and vaccines. Only the very strong had enough natural
resistance to infection to stay healthy on the long voyage.
There were many burials at sea.

The men took turns scrubbing out the living quarters
with strong vinegar solutions. The women struggled to cook
a bit of food out on the open deck. But the tossing of the
ship put out the fire in their stoves, or sent the food flying
across the deck.

They held prayer meetings beseeching God to bring
them safely to shore. As the food ran out and the smell
of impure water became more and more rank, the prayer
meetings were held more frequently. One child fell ill, and
then another. Frightened old people prayed to live long
enough to see land again. The dream of a rich farm in a
new world was replaced by a simple prayer. "Oh Lord, let
me live long enough to be buried in the ground with a
cross to mark my grave."

Only the strong survived. Only the strong could last

days without enough food and fresh water, and they were weakened by the terrible voyage.

It was months before they sighted land; months before they reached the seaports of Quebec or Boston or New York; months of devastating physical hardship and wearying sadness as one and another of their families fell ill.

The sturdy Scandinavians who had so hopefully left their farms and fishing villages were quite changed by the time they reached port. They had spent most of their money getting to the ocean and crossing it. Now they had little or none left. They had spent great quantities of energy on the trip and now there was very little of that left.

At last they had reached the New World. A new world in which they could not even speak the language, where they didn't know the customs or understand the money. Was the kroner a dollar? Or a penny?

They left the ships, carrying their gaily painted trunks, and found themselves in the middle of busy, bustling cities. Where were the farm lands? Who would show them the way? Did they have money enough to continue their trip? Were they still strong enough? No wonder so many other immigrants remained in the very same cities where their ships docked. But the Scandinavians had come with a dream of land. And they would not let go of the dream.

Some men on the docks told them one way to travel, some told them another. They spoke kindly to the travellers and even threw in a word or two of Danish or Swedish. Some men took their money and promised to return with railroad tickets and provisions. They took the money, but did not return.

This had happened to the immigrants before. Travelling across Europe, they had met other petty thieves who lived off the ignorance of the bewildered immigrants.

It would not have been at all hard to sink into hopeless despair, to give up the journey ahead of them, and find jobs as laborers in the city. But they held fast to the land dream. Perhaps it was because they could not possibly imagine the hardships that lay ahead: Perhaps, because there were family or friends waiting for them in Illinois or Kansas or South Dakota, or because they had sold a year's labor in exchange for boat and train tickets to the West.

It might have been the *America Book* the "America letters" and the "America dream" of land, of grain, of cattle, of farms, too beautiful to give up.

CHAPTER V

The Trunk In the Attic

" I went to a port down the coast and took ship for the New World. I was nothing but a boy from the provinces, ignorant of travel. You'll have an idea of the extent of my wardrobe when I tell you that I wore one shirt from Norway to South Dakota. It had its last washing the day before we arrived in New York.

"When I landed in New York things were very different, and the language threw me into terrible confusion. I couldn't speak or understand a word of English. It wasn't until I got aboard the train that I discovered meals weren't furnished with my railroad ticket. By that time, I was down to ten cents in American money and a copper piece from Norway. I went without food for three days and three nights, all the way from New York to South Dakota.

"I left the train at a little station on the Dakota prairie. I saw nothing but level land, like the sea. My uncle did not meet me.

"By this time, the sun was going down. I struck out on foot, soon lost my way, and walked far into the night. It was one of those still prairie nights, breathless with heat. I felt as though I'd been dropped down in the midst of nowhere . . . outside the charmed circle of life.

"If you couldn't conquer that feeling, you were lost indeed."

This is how one young man, Ole Rolvaag, described his arrival in America. He could and did conquer that feeling of being lost, all alone in a strange country. He conquered it well enough to write a masterpiece about it. In his first book, *Letters From America,* he describes the journey. His second book, *Giants In the Earth,* is considered the most fascinating, powerful novel written about pioneer life in the West. It's not just a light-hearted, romantic tale of adventure and conquest, but it does have the romance of truth. It tells of the years of hardship, disappointment and back-breaking labor that had to be endured before the "America dream" could come true.

There were years of loneliness, illness and isolation;

48

years when the pioneers planted crops only to have them torn from the fields by violent windstorms, or frozen by an early cold snap; years when sudden clouds would appear on the horizon, low, menacing, swift-moving. What were these black clouds? They descended in a swoop, thousands upon thousands of voracious grasshoppers. They ate every leaf, every bud, every grain of wheat in sight. They ate the threads off the clothes that were hung out to dry. They ate until nothing at all was left, until the fields were bare, and when they moved on to the next farm they left their eggs behind. Next summer, just as the crops were ripening, the eggs matured and the plague of grasshoppers descended again.

Another year without a harvest, another hungry winter. Why plant? Why not quit and move on, give up the land and try for gold in California? Some did, but most did not. They had already given too much of themselves to turn away now. They had invested their lives in the struggle for land. They would not let the land break them; they would break the land. If they could survive the ocean voyage and the terrible journey west, they could survive another winter.

Ole Rolvaag's account of his trip to South Dakota

in 1896 is grim, even when the railroad provided transportation across the plains. Hundreds of thousands of
earlier immigrants were not so lucky; they had arrived
before the railroad.

After the travellers left their ships in New York, they
walked across the city to the Hudson River where they
boarded a steamer bound for Albany up the Hudson River.
At Albany they changed to a small canal boat which took
them along the Erie Canal to Buffalo.

Here they changed boats again. This time they took
one of the Great Lakes steamers across Lake Erie. The
steamer brought them to Toledo, Ohio. From Toledo
they rode or walked the two hundred miles to Chicago, Illinois. At Chicago they took another Great Lakes steamer
up Lake Michigan to Milwaukee, Wisconsin.

From fjord boat to ocean vessel, from ocean vessel to
canal boat, and from canal boat to Great Lakes steamer —
they changed transportation many times.

Now they needed a covered wagon, a cow and a bull
and, if possible, several chickens before they headed west

again. By this time most of the immigrants were penni-
less. The trip must be postponed awhile in order to earn
some money. There was work in the forests, cutting and
hauling lumber. There was day labor to be found building
houses or laying rail for the new railroad. Women without
young children to care for found jobs as servants. The luck-
iest families were those with grown children; the sons went
out to work with their fathers, and the daughters with their
mothers. They were able to put money aside fairly rapidly
and be on their way again. But for families with young
children, it often took a year or two to save enough for a
covered wagon and provisions for the trip.

Now, came the journey across the prairie and the
search for just the right land. Some of the pioneers planned
to buy government land at $1.25 an acre. Others looked for
homestead sites (land that was free to anyone who would
cultivate it).

No wonder it took three years from the time the
Sorensens left Norway until they were settled in their first
sod hut on their own land. Despite hunger and cold, crop

failure and grasshopper plague, they would not leave. If they could last this long, they could last a little longer.

They thought of their sturdy Viking ancestors, Leif Ericson and his crew. Almost a thousand years ago, these Scandinavian explorers were the first Europeans to set foot in the New World. They risked a perilous voyage over unknown waters to discover a new land. Now their descendants would tame some of this land.

Where once there was nothing but open, desolate prairie, there are now miles and miles of rich farm land. Bit by bit, the frontier was pushed back. Family after family claimed a piece of land, and cultivated it.

They learned not to plant too early in the spring because a touch of winter frost might return to kill the seed. They discovered that smoke and fire would rid them of grasshoppers. They found they could not wait too late in autumn to harvest their grain. One cold night might kill the crop.

The years of back-breaking labor were over. The land was theirs and the harvest was good. When the railroad came they were able to sell their crops and ship them across the country. They now had money to build handsome frame houses.

Today the windows of these prosperous homes look out over acres and acres of beautiful grain fields. And up in the attic there is often a trunk stored away — a gaily painted trunk, made of strong lumber and decorated with birds and leaves and flowers. Across the top, a name is boldly printed. Perhaps it's Pedersen or Johnsson or Fjellstedt. Surely, it's the name of people who endured the struggle to make the "America dream" come true.

CHAPTER VI

Improved Farm Land

Tall timber stood here once,
    here on a corn belt along the Monon.
Here the roots of a half mile of trees
    dug their runners deep in the loam
    for a grip and a hold against windstorms.
Then the axmen came and the chips flew
    to the zing of steel and handle —
    the land railsplitters cut the big ones first,
    the beeches and the oaks, then the brush.
Dynamite, wagons and houses took the stumps —
    the plows sink their teeth in —
    now it is first-class corn land — improved property —
    and the hogs grunt over the fodder crops.
It would come hard now for this half mile of improved
    farm land
    along the Monon corn belt,
    on a piece of Grand Prairie,
    to remember once it had a great singing family of trees.[*]

This is a poem written by Carl Sandburg about the
land on which he grew up.

The son of a poor Swedish immigrant who could barely sign his name and could read only a word or two from the Bible, Carl Sandburg became one of America's greatest writers. His poems are songs in praise of America — the land and the people. The cornhuskers, the housewives in their kitchens, the farm and the farm animals, the simple prairie life was beautiful to him. He saw poetry in the people and heard music in the wind whipping the prairie grass. His poems seemed to sing, themselves. Sandburg took to wandering around the country, a kind of modern-day troubadour, reciting his verses while he strummed the mandolin.

His joy in America, its people and its limitless possibilities, led him to become more and more interested in the life of one American — Abraham Lincoln. In 1940 Carl Sandburg's four-volume biography of Lincoln, *The Prairie Years* and *The War Years*, won the Pulitzer Prize. It is considered one of the finest biographies ever written.

Sandburg, like most children of Scandinavian immigrants, worked on a farm while he was growing up. But he tried other things, too. He worked as a bootblack, dishwasher, salesman, barber, milk truck driver and a dozen other things so that he could earn his college tuition.

Every immigrant group escaping poverty in Europe has understood the value of an education. At home they were denied the opportunity to learn to read and write. In the old country a good education was a privilege reserved for noblemen and rich men. But how could a poor man improve his condition without an education? How could he learn a trade or a profession? How could he hope to give his children a better life than his parents were able to give him?

In America, where there were no noblemen and no privileged few, even a poor, illiterate, newly-arrived immigrant could plan for his children's education. Once the first hard years were over, when stomachs were full and there was time to spare, he thought about the future. The years ahead belonged to the children. If they were to make the most of them, they must go to school.

For the Scandinavian settlers, the years brought prosperity. With each successive harvest, the farms grew richer. Land they had gotten free, or bought at $1.25 an acre, went up in value until now it sells for thousands of dollars an acre.

Machines were invented that helped the farmer cultivate more land. The tractor, the thresher and the plough could each do the work of ten men. Now the children could be spared (except perhaps at harvest time) to go to school. Soon the prairie was dotted with thriving towns, each with its own school. Some children walked several miles to school each day. Others lived so far away, they had to stay in boarding houses in town during the week in order to attend school. Since the Scandinavian immigrants believed firmly in free public education, they sent their children to the town schools. Here they met children of other nationalities and religious faiths. They learned to speak English and began to adopt American ways. Santa Claus, not the Yule Buck, brought their presents on Christmas Eve. They celebrated the Fourth of July and taught their parents why.

The older people began to wish that they, too, could learn the history of their adopted homeland. In town after town, the school lights were seen blazing way into the night. Farmers and their wives, the day's work done, were hard at work again. They were learning to read and write English. They studied math and history. They grabbed at the opportunity that had once been denied them — the opportunity to learn. The Adult Education Program was begun by Scandinavian immigrants.

They built Augustana College, Adolphus College, Bethany College, Luther College, North Park College, Bethel Seminary and Upsala College. Thousands of engineers, doctors, lawyers and teachers were taught their professions at these schools.

Norwegians, fisher-folk by tradition, helped build the American fishing industry. The Danes became the backbone of the American dairy industry. The Swedes planted and harvested huge crops of grain.

A young Danish immigrant, Jacob Riis, became one of America's most passionate crusaders for free, compulsory education. Riis, a newspaper reporter, arrived in New York in 1870. He saw what was happening to the immigrants who remained in the city. They lived in filthy, crowded tenements and worked long hours for very little money. At home the women and children did "piece-work," bits and pieces that could be brought from the factory and worked on at home. The children did not go to school. They didn't even have time to play.

Riis was outraged at what he saw and, with his newspaper articles, helped arouse the rest of the nation. Laws were passed to eliminate overcrowded tenements, to im-

prove safety conditions in factories, and to abolish child
labor. Like so many of his countrymen, Riis was a pioneer;
but his struggle was in the conquering of poverty rather
than land.

Scandinavians have been elected governors in several western states and have been sent to Washington as senators and congressmen. There have been prominent architects, builders, athletes, designers, and scientists of Scandinavian descent. They have contributed to the arts, science, and business. There is actually no phase of American life which has not been enriched by the Scandinavian-Americans. The farmers' sons found their way into every possible career and profession.

INDEX